BALIKBAYAN

Like its namesake, *Balikbayan* holds dear life's extraordinary essentials. Which is to say, this is a collection of shape-shifting care packages: poems as reminders of what sustains us; poems that bear witness to needful defiance; poems of generosity and grit. As Audre Lorde would "make, demand, translate" everyday beauty to build an "arsenal against despair," Dujie Tahat transfigures hand-me-downs and home-made remixes, "bright trinkets" and love notes and wildflowers. How fortunate we are to read these gifts—to be carried safely beyond "...The Unfathomable News That Every Thing We've Ever Known Will Shortly Be On Fire" toward new dreams, new forms. **R.A. VILLANUEVA**

For so many Filipinx, balikbayan boxes are totemic. Though we rarely name it as such, the ritual filling of these boxes is an object lesson in diaspora, empire, and the immigrant homesickness that defies English translation. With the same reverent attention to structure, Dujie Tahat unpacks balikbayan—an identity so crammed with questions and contradictions that it might never find a true home, but can find peace in the searching. I love these poems. They are pasalubong from that distant cousin who somehow knows you as intimately as you know yourself. **ANGELA GARBES**

In Dujie Tahat's latest work, they speak of a longing that cannot merely be erased through the accumulation of things. Tahat questions our insistence in the economy of our grief by constructing delicate, jewel-like memory boxes. And in the moment when we open these gifts, we are offered a chance to return to a home that is within ourselves. Within each balikbayan box, the poems extend a hand, beckoning us to also pack a little of ourselves as we revisit the sources of our longings, whether they be the immediacy of familial crisis, the deep trauma of a lost world, or a moment of recognition in the archives of our imagination. **OLIVER DE LA PAZ**

How much can be said before a box is packed? And how much before it is unpacked? Reading Dujie Tahat's *Balikbayan* is a synesthetic experience. Every line folds and unfolds on its scores, revealing each poem's crisp and dolorous music. This collection is an innovative wonder—to borrow Tahat's words, here there are "no blemishes." Only "bloom." **JANINE JOSEPH**

In *Balikbayan*, Dujie Tahat creates a form that enacts a consecration of both a container and an enactment of love within the Filipinx/a/o diaspora. With invention and verve, Tahat packs and packs each balikbayan box to gift us history and tsimis and music and grief, memory and flowers and anger and forgiveness and legacy. These boxes are of and for kasama and pamilya—not limited by borders or time or space. Instead, Tahat crafts universes inside these seemingly mundane, seemingly small receptacles, which grow bigger on the inside, ever-expanding with "a more tender touching," one that "could stuff a whole mosque in—a cathedral, too." **MICHELLE PEÑALOZA**

Balikbayan is a gorgeous legacy of connectedness to one's self. To fill and deliver a balikbayan box is to build connective tissue across an ocean and to return home bearing gifts. This is precisely and magnificently what Dujie Tahat does in this collection; fills and delivers their story; building the connection across the complexity of living in multiple identities and finding home in ourselves. What Dujie Tahat is able to do with multiple languages (English, Tagalog, Taglish, Hip Hop) is surreal and only further proves this entanglement that only they are able to deliver so gracefully. One of the most compelling collections of poetry I've ever come across. **EBO BARTON**

BALIKBAYAN

■

DUJIE TAHAT

NEW MICHIGAN PRESS
TUCSON, ARIZONA

NEW MICHIGAN PRESS
DEPT OF ENGLISH, P. O. BOX 210067
UNIVERSITY OF ARIZONA
TUCSON, AZ 85721-0067

<http://newmichiganpress.com>

Orders and queries to <nmp@thediagram.com>.

Copyright © 2022 by Dujie Tahat.
All rights reserved.

ISBN 978-1-934832-86-8. FIRST PRINTING.

Cover design by Janelle Quibuyen. Interior design by Ander Monson.

CONTENTS

Balikbayan Naman   1

American Balikbayan   2

Balikbayan Filled With Theory   3

I Put The Pieces Of A Failed Sestina In The Balikbayan As Packing Peanuts To Hold What I Really Won In The Divorce Which Is Not Yours To Know   6

While Recording Bars In The Studio That Is Really Just A Souped Up Balikbayan In His Mama's Backyard I Try Explaining To The Homie Why Filipinos Love Chaka Khan Which Is How I Know The Sample To Kanye West's "Through The Wire"   7

When You Finally Empty The Balikbayan You'll Wanna Press In From The Corners   8

Fragile: Balikbayan In My Frightened & Naked Arms   9

Birthday Balikbayan   10

Nayabkilab Or In Taglish Sometimes You Reverse The Syllabic Order Of Everyday Words For Effect   11

Despite What I Know Of Death & Its Grip On What Grows I Fill This Balikbayan With Flowers Anyway   12

My Mother Made My Science Fair Projects Sometimes But Instead Of Trifolds Would Cut Out The Sides Of A Balikbayan   13

Every Balikbayan Is In One Way Or Another For My Mother   **14**

Another Balikbayan In Which Ma Asks Her Kids To Go To Mass With Her Pero No One Ever Does   **15**

Once Again I Find Myself In The Homie's Ma's Backyard Unpacking Balikbayan Bars This Time Filled With Hoop Dreams   **16**

Balikbayan For My Step-Sister For The First & Only Time We Met   **17**

No Balikbayan Is Large Enough To Place The Unfathomable News That Every Thing We've Ever Known Will Shortly Be On Fire   **18**

Balikbayan In Praise Of Impending Irreversible Ecological Disaster   **19**

Notes   **21**

Acknowledgements   **23**

BALIKBAYAN NAMAN

I swear I could stuff a whole mosque in—a cathedral, too. Maybe even a white t shirt & a pair of blue jeans or two. Ship this shibboleth across the ocean for cuz just cuz. Count all this here rent money & tell me why I shouldn't. Haven't checked my mail in months. I'm eating Frosted Flakes for lunch & my voicemail is full. My taxes are overdue once again, but watch me flex. & still they say I'm un-American! That I'll never understand what it means to overpour & overstuff & over the edges of the brim—beyond what I could even imagine—overstate the obvious.

AMERICAN BALIKBAYAN

I wrap each useless bauble & bright trinket in sheaves of Emerson's self-reliance & JSTOR packets exploring the origin of American individualism in all its smoke. That is not the vehicle but the tenor. The jeepney is how our people boil flesh in its own blood for feast, solder guns out of scrap metal spark, make mothers & sisters our greatest export. What caribou shit is this in the middle of the road. That whiff of new money. Yes, it's both General Patton's pipe & a pair of fake Prada shoes. It feeds. It is whatever the hell I say it is & like ma says, it'll need a lot more patis.

BALIKBAYAN FILLED WITH THEORY

In the field of political communications it is widely understood that when an argument is presented in the negative, what is remembered is that which was negated. As in: I am not a human. It does not have to be said. Liberties are not taken. This is not a costume. I am not a poppy in November nor a hellhound wildfire in May. No, the coffers are not empty. The rich are not gnawing the gristle off the bone, they don't not care. Hours later on a toilet made of not-gold, they don't suck the fat from below their fingernails, not almost tallow now, not a mouth evinced of smoke.

■

                the   cat

                                    ate
                              t h   e
                                    cost

                                 of   a
           c   r   o   w
                                          Hours later
              a   n
                       heir   nails   a
low   vi ce

                              ■

Ga]the[ring about,   the dislo]cat[ed
& the dispossessed
play pusoy dos   to pass
the time.   I sk]ate [toward it, even
calculate omw]   t h e
                       cost   [of a kick-
                                          flip.
[Tbh an opportunity al]of[t]   a[nd I
    s] c   r   o [ll] w[ith both fingers,
thumb a royal flush, so the] Hours later
[fray at] a   [han[d b]old[er than its holder
sharpens sight. T]heir [wet]nails [so] a [k
in] low [stakes,   bad ad] vi ce [& gin.]

I PUT THE PIECES OF A FAILED SESTINA IN THE BALIKBAYAN AS PACKING PEANUTS TO HOLD WHAT I REALLY WON IN THE DIVORCE WHICH IS NOT YOURS TO KNOW

The kids grieving summer was a joke. All heavy-breathing heaving. You asked: What? I lied: Nothing. So leaving seemed right next. I left but was bluffing. I grieved the score. I dry heaved for months. The kids love Christmas twice as much now but posturing means the oldest grieves openly. We do nothing. We are nothing but a pair of heart muscles heaving old blood to new & here, I thought leaving meant no more lies, no more leaving. That which is not-grief I heave over the bluff along with love's other leave-behinds. No, no, no things grieve like we do.

WHILE RECORDING BARS IN THE STUDIO THAT IS REALLY JUST A SOUPED UP BALIKBAYAN IN HIS MA'S BACKYARD I TRY EXPLAINING TO THE HOMIE WHY FILIPINOS LOVE CHAKA KHAN WHICH IS HOW I KNOW THE SAMPLE TO KANYE WEST'S "THROUGH THE WIRE"

Got it from Dilla, go figure. Bass-creepin ninja guerilla. I'm more ether than you think & I got no greed card. Meanwhile, polis bright lights ask who we are. This lyric not for you, sir, more for both my diasporas—those Arabicas & Filipinas—only a permanent revolution will free us. Crusade new place on a brutal, feudal Tuesday. My grandpapa's grandpapa ask his friend Ahmed, *Who they?* Hellish mans with metal hands fetish lands then forget it. My kasamas wear designer. My mama don't regret it. I said it so I meant it, but maybe I did embellish—

WHEN YOU FINALLY EMPTY THE BALIKBAYAN YOU'LL WANNA PRESS IN FROM THE CORNERS

Lay the last box flat, a temporary area rug for your first apartment. Don't even got a futon & the IKEA bookshelf still needing to be assembled. Stir in the Ichiban packet last, finish it with the Maggi, a drop of sesame oil if you can find it. A bowl of any broth is healing. This is the last time the walls will be this white. Air your dirty laundry. So much space. Wow, you really only own books & clothes. Your kids got no toys. They sleep on your floor-mattress. At some point you'll get bowls. At some point you'll have to sweep the kitchen. At some point the kids will leave.

FRAGILE: BALIKBAYAN IN MY FRIGHTENED & NAKED ARMS

He drops the S in *SCOOP & KICK!* at his first swim lesson the night before. *Grip tight,* says his teacher. *Twenty-five pounds acts different in the water.* When mom calls the next day, he's already broken his arm. For some reason, I imagine blood. Then science: ulnar fracture, olecranon hook. A thousand times I've looked at my body in the mirror before he wakes. I'm pleased that I'm pleased that it's still growing too. I make room. *No self-hate today, myself.* I examine my son's arms only to find they look nothing like mine—no blemishes where I'd expect them to bloom.

BIRTHDAY BALIKBAYAN

A dress on a body with a face that breaks into a smile like mine. My little stick figure boy. My son, hot-headed in the yellow sun. Fuming at the tips of your fingers right before the turn of the magic trick. Conjurer. Illusionist. Take a bread loaf then make a thief. This wave, then—look!—you in the eye of a crow. Were that you only ever bud but no. O bud. To observe you bloom. What unforgivable cruelty to imagine you turn, wrinkle, go to seed. I will long have been at sea or so they say. Let me get to it then: I will die & what I would give to unknow that you will too.

NAYABKILAB OR IN TAGLISH SOMETIMES YOU REVERSE THE SYLLABIC ORDER OF EVERYDAY WORDS FOR EFFECT

For example: Golets! from Let's go! One can reverse the letters, too. As in: American Lodi! No matter how far away I am from the landhome, I'm a good yob. When making nayabkilab, it doesn't matter which of the nine sides rests on the motbot. If that's confusing, it's kayo. Remember, like any argot, Tagalog-English slang has a public language from which it bases its grammatical & syntactical rules. Destroy all lodis. Kcuf the lispu. Does this make sense yet? I'm Noypi & Abar & maybe even Canieram. I'm senglot. Susmariosep, I'm stumbling. Gone.

DESPITE WHAT I KNOW OF DEATH & ITS GRIP ON WHAT GROWS I FILL THIS BALIKBAYAN WITH FLOWERS ANYWAY

If a leaf falls early, my mother propagates it, green thumbs the thing into a new pot, so the whole windowsill jadejadejadejadejadejadejadejade. We moved into a house fenced in with lilaclaclaclaclaclaclilaclaclacs pushed up against the roseoseoseoseoseohiphips. We planned a garden. The rhododendendronononononondron overgrew. An empty plot rots. No friends. We're the wildest. I cut villains out of dogogogogogwood, I mistook hyahyahyahyahyacinth for honeyneyneyneysucsuckle. What I know about flowers fills a starter home. Across, over: a verve, aberrant life—

MY MOTHER MADE MY SCIENCE FAIR PROJECTS SOMETIMES BUT INSTEAD OF TRIFOLDS WOULD CUT OUT THE SIDES OF A BALIKBAYAN

I trace red-dotted ovals around my obliques & inner thighs. This—my child-mind intimates—is where the doctor will cut the fat. I played at being small, but my body stayed my body. This isn't theater. I don't need to see the gun to know it goes off. My oldest daughter gets cast as the Queen of Hearts in her school's rendition of *Alice in Wonderland*. She wants to be off-book by the end of winter break. Climbing the stairs in the dark, I step on Optimus Prime's dino-sword. I yell at no one. The kids have left. I swipe at my phone & ma steps back to survey her work.

EVERY BALIKBAYAN IS IN ONE WAY OR ANOTHER FOR MY MOTHER

Forgiveness is laborious that way. A never-ending line of empty boxes so long, we forget—I pin my awards to the fat bellies of stars. She pulls stitches from the spaces between. The thread is black, the point sharp. The odds are astronomical we'd end up, here, on the other side of our pale blue dot like this, at opposing ends of the cheap azure rug bought on clearance at Ross last week to cover up the fireplace burns of escaped embers. It's been at least a year. Finally dry enough to start, we throw in the kindling. Where there is smoke, I finally say I love you.

ANOTHER BALIKBAYAN IN WHICH MA ASKS HER KIDS TO GO TO MASS WITH HER PERO NO ONE EVER DOES

So in went the Word—for it was the first day. The second, Father was away. My mother folded the hand-me-downs slowly to form perfect angles. The basket full of fluorescent squares. The box solid. She could reach the rafters during the hymnal. Every day of the week there are candles to light. I do the dishes. I know I need a more tender touching. I moisturize. I pack lunches with tiny notes in them for the next day. Love letters for my little ones. Send them each off to school armed without so much as a straight line but a loosely spun doodle of a boy holding a bear.

ONCE AGAIN I FIND MYSELF IN THE HOMIE'S MA'S BACKYARD UNPACKING BALIKBAYAN BARS THIS TIME FILLED WITH HOOP DREAMS

Under the sun & in the rain of a wet runner, rim-stuntin finger roll hummin, gold in my mouth cuz it's the golden hour. I'm holdin out till I'm holdin power—up in my maw, between my jaws. Oh my God. I'm snatchin the ball. Call me The Claw. Clock on the wall tick tocks. My hip pops. You pissed off. I pick pocks. I hit rainbow drip drops. My shit knocks. My shot wet. My socks smell. My drop step look like 'o1 Duncan & I'm still runnin with this dead leg. I'm not young, but I'm not not no old head. Object permanence —whoa!—makes no sense—

BALIKBAYAN FOR MY STEP-SISTER FOR THE FIRST & ONLY TIME WE MET

Sorry I made you cry. I was crying, too, at your door in your crying father's arms. I didn't know you'd be there. I was yelling when I hung up on pops last. A weaker connection. A crack in a golden Beamer's windshield. A hairline. Then all at once black & yellow static slid into the astonished gap between his lips. Not a word since. What else have I been silent about? To whom? I have to say: I love you. It's almost impossible to believe. My son is your age; my youngest, your sister's. In my bed they still sleep, so some nights when I rise, it's from your dreams.

NO BALIKBAYAN IS LARGE ENOUGH TO PLACE THE UNFATHOMABLE NEWS THAT EVERY THING WE'VE EVER KNOWN WILL SHORTLY BE ON FIRE

Meet Moh. Meet Jun Jun & Samira. At this moment there are more than two dozen revolutions occurring around the globe in Chile, Lebanon, Hong Kong, France, Sudan. Fati posts updates. Agnes tends to the wounded. The Philippines has been protesting their president since his inauguration. Del makes another hand gun. Everyone demonstrates. Flint you know pero there are hoods in capitals without access to clean water. Power is the thread through it all. Of course, my old boss (the progressive one) asked, on my last day, what the point is in naming our failures.

BALIKBAYAN IN PRAISE OF IMPENDING IRREVERSIBLE ECOLOGICAL DISASTER

Art-making isn't suffering until it is. After a good day of writing, I don't enjoy it. The world is so strange until I remember I'm going to die. Then it's beautiful. Over a barren hill is a rainbow, a gesture towards artifice. The wasps that die for fig to fruit in a poem I write are no metaphor. The planet is unbeauty. I've been divorced. Sure, my pops beat me. I've failed my children & several other beloveds. The room spins. I am so afraid is a confession too. The world is _____ & men in uniforms would happily kill me depending on what side of the orchard I stay.

NOTES

Balikbayans are large boxes sent home to the Philippines often filled with gifts to signal a kind of repatriation. The biggest Filipinx export is its people, & balikbayan boxes have historically enjoyed tax- & duty-free privileges, making them a popular—& sometimes, the only economically feasible—way to stay connected to family & friends. The passage of the Patriot Act in 2001, however, dramatically increased the U.S. Department of Homeland Security's scrutiny of the practice, doubling shipment time, increasing costs, & resulting in broken & damaged goods. Over 12 million citizens of the Philippines (or more than ten percent of the islands' population) migrate to another country. It is estimated that over 400,000 balikbayan boxes are sent back home every month.

ACKNOWLEDGMENTS

Big gratitude to the editors of the following publications where many of the poems in this manuscript—sometimes in earlier drafts—first appear or are forthcoming: *Across The Margins, Apogee, Beacon, FlyPaper Lit, Juked, Pacifica Literary Review, Sonora Review, Strange Horizons, The Boiler, The Margins (AAWW), Tiltwest,* and *Washington Square Review.* "American Balikbayan" also appears in the chapbook *Here I Am O My God.* And "Once Again I Find Myself in the Homie's Backyard..." appears on Instagram @4BarFriday

Gratitude to the New Michigan Press team for turning these small boxes into a real book.

A special thanks to the Center for the Book Arts and Simone White for recognizing this book as an honoree. A particular and effusive thanks to artist Oswaldo Garcia for the broadside—what a gift to be seen by you and for the work to be interpreted by your artistic vision.

This book, its form, and all my writing is, in one way or another, my reaching for and a product of community. Those I owe are too many to name.

A few include my mother, my grandmother, my aunts and uncles, Ebo Barton, Angela Garbes, Michelle Peñaloza, Oliver de la Paz, R.A. Villanueva, Gabrielle Bates, Luther Hughes, Rick Barot, Bill Carty, Troy Osaki, Daemond Arrindell, Amaud Jamaul Johnson, Kaveh Akbar, Matthew Olzmann, Kabel Mishka Ligot, Emily Luan, Megan Pinto, Michael Dhyne, Charlotte Abotsi, and Laurel Chen.

A bottomless well of gratitude to Emily Parzybok, my first reader, champion, co-conspirator, dance partner, co-parent, and best friend. Thank you.

This work—as all the work is—is for Isabella, Maximus, and Maya. I love you.

DUJIE TAHAT is a Filipino-Jordanian immigrant living in Washington state. They are the author of the chapbooks *Here I Am O My God*, selected for a Poetry Society of America Chapbook Fellowship; *Salat*, winner of the Tupelo Press Sunken Garden Chapbook Award and longlisted for the 2020 PEN/Voelcker Award for Poetry Collection; and *Balikbayan*, finalist for the New Michigan Press / *DIAGRAM* chapbook contest and Center for Book Arts honoree. Along with Luther Hughes and Gabrielle Bates, they cohost *The Poet Salon* podcast. Find out more about them at DUJIETAHAT.COM.

■

COLOPHON

Text is set in a digital version of Jenson, designed by Robert Slimbach in 1996, and based on the work of punchcutter, printer, and publisher Nicolas Jenson. The titles here are in Futura.

■

NEW MICHIGAN PRESS, based in Tucson, Arizona, prints poetry and prose chapbooks, especially work that transcends traditional genre. Together with DIAGRAM, NMP sponsors a yearly chapbook competition.

DIAGRAM, a journal of text, art, and schematic, is published bimonthly at THEDIAGRAM.COM. Periodic print anthologies are available from the New Michigan Press at NEWMICHIGANPRESS.COM.

www.ingramcontent.com/pod-product-compliance
Lightning Source LLC
Chambersburg PA
CBHW031507040426
42444CB00007B/1246